A JOURNEY TO WORK FROM HOME DURING COVID-19

PANDEMIC LOCKDOWN. WILL IT STILL BE RELEVANT AFTER THE PANDEMIC?

Dr Sulaiman Baputey Ph.D

PARTRIDGE

Copyright © 2021 by Dr Sulaiman Baputey Ph.D.

Library of Congress Control Number:		2021906410
ISBN:	Hardcover	978-1-5437-6414-7
	Softcover	978-1-5437-6413-0
	eBook	978-1-5437-6415-4

All rights reserved. No part of this book may be used or reproduced by any means, graphic, electronic, or mechanical, including photocopying, recording, taping or by any information storage retrieval system without the written permission of the author except in the case of brief quotations embodied in critical articles and reviews.

Because of the dynamic nature of the Internet, any web addresses or links contained in this book may have changed since publication and may no longer be valid. The views expressed in this work are solely those of the author and do not necessarily reflect the views of the publisher, and the publisher hereby disclaims any responsibility for them.

Print information available on the last page.

To order additional copies of this book, contact
Toll Free +65 3165 7531 (Singapore)
Toll Free +60 3 3099 4412 (Malaysia)
orders.singapore@partridgepublishing.com

www.partridgepublishing.com/singapore

To my late parents
for raising me tirelessly
To my wife and children
for making me believe anything is possible during
the COVID-19 pandemic lockdown

When work enters the home forcefully ... The boundary became permeable ... Push employees to shift their mental domains radically ... During the unfortunate COVID-19 pandemic lockdown ...
　　　　　　　　—Dr. Sulaiman Baputey, March 2021

CONTENTS

Preface xiii
Acknowledgments xix

Chapter 1: Working from Home—Current Reality and the Future Work Landscape after COVID-19 Pandemic Lockdown 1
Chapter 2: COVID-19—Disease Trajectory, Virus Characteristics, and Prevention Strategies 8
Chapter 3: Global Reactions to COVID-19 Pandemic—Are They in the Same Boat? 21
Chapter 4: Implications, Challenges, and Advantages during COVID-19 Pandemic Lockdown 27
Chapter 5: Nature and Characteristics of Working from Home during Pre-COVID-19 and Post-COVID-19 Era. What Makes the Difference? 42
Chapter 6: Is Work from Home Favor to Every Task, Occupation, Sector, and Country during COVID-19 Pandemic Lockdown? 50
Chapter 7: The Challenges of Working from Home during COVID-19 Pandemic Lockdown 60

Chapter 8:   The Privileges of Working from Home
             during COVID-19 Pandemic Lockdown.............68
Chapter 9:   Digital Technology as a Magic Bullet for
             Performing Work from Home during
             COVID-19 Pandemic Lockdown........................75
Chapter 10: Work-from-Home Policy and Employees'
             Job Manual—a Practical Guideline for
             Human Resource Managers and Employees.......85

List of Tables

Table 5.1: The Summary of Major Differences between
           Pre-COVID-19 Working from Home and
           Post-COVID-19 Working from Home 48
Table 6.1: Summary of Tasks that Can Be Done from
           Home and Cannot Be Done from Home 53
Table 6.2: Occupation Characteristics that Do and Do
           Not Favor to Work from Home 55
Table 6.3: Potential Share of Time Spent Working from
           Home by Sectors 57

List of Abbreviations

AIDS: Acquired Immune Deficiency Syndrome
COVID-19 – Coronavirus Disease 19
CMCO: Conditional Mobility Control Order
EMCO: Enhanced Mobility Control Order
HIV: Human Immunodeficiency Virus
MCO: Mobility Control Order
MERS: Middle East Respiratory Syndrome
OPEC: Organization of Petroleum Exporting Countries
SARS: Severe Acute Respiratory Syndrome
US: United State of America
PHEIC: Public Health of Emergency of International Concern
WHO: World Health Organization

Preface

Old Normal, New Normal, and Next Normal of Working from Home

The term *working from home* has been used interchangeably with many variations in human resource literature and practices. Among the variations included are *teleworking, telecommuting, working from remote, digital work connectivity, virtual working, working without office, flexible working hours, fluid working conditions, work from anywhere,* and lately, *hybrid working conditions.*

Although many variations have been used arbitrarily, the core operational definition remains: work arrangement that allows employees to execute work tasks from home during some or all portion of the working week using information and communication technologies (ICT).

Tracing back the history on how work from home evolved in human resource literature, it was adopted in 1973, when

OPEC imposed embargo on oil price, which triggered the price acceleration in the market. The increases in oil prices had made commuting cost for employees more expensive and therefore pushed oil companies to change from traditional and collocated work policy to work-from-home policy, which allowed employees to work remotely.

The recent mandated initiative from the authority, which pushes employees to work from home, however, does not happen in a vacuum. It was greatly triggered by the COVID-19 pandemic lockdown coupled with digital technological advancement in personal computer, the internet, email, broadband connectivity, laptops, smartphone, cloud computing, teleconferencing, Zoom, Google Meet, and recently, artificial intelligence and robotics.

Chronologically, the evolution of the work-from-home model can be divided into three critical phases: old normal phase, which occurred before COVID-19; new-normal phase, which occurred during COVID-19; and next-normal phase, which is expected to occur after the COVID-19 pandemic is over. While the old normal before COVID-19 fully geared employees to work from office, the new normal during COVID-19 fully geared employees to work from home. The next normal, however, will be more relaxed in which it will geared employees to work partially from home and partially from the office—which is popularly known as the *hybrid work model* among human resource scholars and practitioners.

Highlighting the future of working from home, many human resource experts, organizations, researchers, and scholars predicted it will still continue even after the pandemic is over as long as social interaction remains an occupational disease issue that blocks employees to work from office premises.

As a result, the heyday for those employees who were physically reporting to an office with complete apparel—such as double-breasted jacket, shining shoes, elegant necktie, and smart briefcase—every day of the workweek is not likely to resume. Adding further on the sad news to office enthusiasts, the next *hybrid work model* will not be easily reversed into fully geared working from office, which has been enjoyed by them over the decades before the COVID-19 pandemic.

The *hybrid work model* that allows employees to split their time between the office and home is expected to become the next normal during the corporate reopening. Elaborating further the *hybrid return-to-work model,* it will be top of mind among many employers and employees and will be solidly taking shape after the pandemic is over. To be certain, most of the employees will be in a *hybrid* workforce permanently, which allows them to choose which day of the week they want to work from office and which day of the week they want to work from home.

Additionally, the next normal of *hybrid work model* brings several other advantages, such as it is key to understand the more flexible future of work, which encompasses many possible systems. It is more freedom, which allows employees to choose where and when to work. It gives more autonomy to employees to fit work around the rest of their lives. Ideally, the next normal of *hybrid work model* is the best of both worlds, structure and sociability on one hand and flexibility and independence on the other hand.

Detailing further on the beauty of the next normal of *hybrid work model*, it is designed in such a way that certain days are block for in-office meetings and collaboration and remote days for work involving individual focus. Employees' induction program, team building, and new product development kickoffs may require employees' physical presence in the office premises but not necessarily for other works.

The proportion between working from home and working from office, however, received mix reactions from the employees. In one pilot survey, which studied the proportion of working days between home and office, more than half of the employees prefer working from home three days a week while the rest of the days working from office. Contrarily in another study among executive level employees, they think employees should be working from office at least three days a week to maintain a strong corporate culture. They are of the opinion that company corporate culture cannot survive by allowing employees to work from home more than three days a week.

The option to go for *hybrid work model* also received mix response from employers. Quoting a survey on Malaysian employers' readiness to implement the hybrid work model, while government sector is fully geared to implement the hybrid work model in the future, private sectors prefer employees to return to office as soon as possible. This is due to the fact that working from home is not part of Malaysian private sectors' culture. However, it is again dependent on the sentiment and mentality of their bosses.

The implementation of the *hybrid work model* is expected to bring new challenges and implication on employment law landscape, particularly on employees' working hours in the office premises. The employees' mandated minimum working hours in the office will no longer be applied; therefore, this working hour conditions is expected to change with the new hybrid model. The new working hours law must be clear about how it should be implemented.

Dr. Sulaiman Baputey, PhD (Talent Management)
March 2021

Acknowledgments

What and Who Triggered Me to Author This Book

There are many factors that pushed me to bring this book into reality. Among the factors included is my specific background in human resources, not only as a senior lecturer, trainer, and coach but also my practical involvement in drafting multiple domains of talent management policies such as talent attraction, talent selection, talent development, talent rewards, talent assessment, talent engagement, and talent retentions. A special thanks goes to my former employer, MARA Poly-Tech University College, Malaysia, who gave me an opportunity to explore this field; my PhD supervisor, Dr. Sheikh Muhamad Hizam Sheikh Khairuddin, from Universiti Kuala Lumpur who polished and shined my human resource knowledge; and consulting organizations who turned me into a human resource specialist. Their contributions have shifted my thinking horizon particularly in bringing this book to life.

Highlighting the uniqueness of this book, it is rare in human resource practice and literature, which is not only able to diagnose the current implication of working from home during the pandemic lockdown but also able to imagine its future work landscape—which somehow is still puzzling and uncertain even after all the employees are vaccinated and the pandemic is over.

However, the great factor that really triggered me to author this book is the mandated pandemic lockdown during COVID-19 causality. While many people viewed the pandemic lockdown as a catastrophe and peril that pushed them to isolate themselves at home with a lot of negative energies—such as family distraction, anxiety, mental disorder, trauma, lonely, insomnia, and exhaustion—in contrast, it gives me a lot of leisure, pleasure, calmness, and opportunities to complete my mission in successfully publishing this book—and certainly with the support from Partridge Publishing.

Finally, I also would like to express my gratitude to my family members for their love and support in understanding the long hours and the sacrificed weekends.

Chapter 1

Working from Home—Current Reality and the Future Work Landscape after COVID-19 Pandemic Lockdown

The year 2020 has been game changing for the new-millennium workplace. It has brought about *radical shift* in the place we work—from luxury and spacious office setting into work from home. This shift is expected to stay until a period that we are still uncertain of. With the constrained occasioned by COVID-19, working from home and technology solution became imperative. Even as the prospects of vaccine become imminent, working from home will shape the workplace of the future.

Without a doubt, 2020 will go down as the master of work from home. As the world recovers from the pandemic, there is a silver lining in the work-from-home trend. The work-from-home measure that is enforced in response to the COVID-19 pandemic will continue to have huge bearing on workplace policies, practices, and behaviors in 2021.

Tracing back the work trajectory, before Wuhan became pandemic city, those employees fond of their pajamas have—for decades—argued that a lot of work that is done in the office could be better done at home. With the outbreak of COVID-19, their ideas were put to the test in a large scale. The result shows that yes, a lot of work can be done at home. As a result, work from home is now no longer a perk for some employees, where only certain top echelon in the organization has the opportunity to enjoy it before the COVID-19 pandemic. It is now becoming a necessity, and many employees seem to prefer doing it.

The effectiveness of work from home has been a debated topic for decades even before the pandemic. Although the original intentions of working from home is to curb the spread of COVID-19, it has brought many challenges. In reality, there are many challenges discovered during the implementation of working from home. However, the most critical challenges include low productivity, limited career prospect, haywire office space, distraction from family members, blurred line between the domain of home and office, and the most serious implication, multiple mental sufferings.

Explaining further on the sad side of working from home, it has shut office doors and sent staff home. Similarly, employees are facing months away from their desks. In the extreme condition, work from home also has pushed almost every employee from busy office environment to silent home office. The most dramatic implication is working from home has changed the aura of dwelling from living and resting space into official home office.

Along the line, working from home has created many new norms and has shifted employees' work behavior, which challenges conventional human resource practices in the world of work. There is no more morning ring, there is no more traffic jam, there is no more driving to office, there is no more rushing back to home, and there is no more travel and petrol cost. More surprisingly, there is no more clock in and clock out, a formal human resource norm that has been practiced to measure availability of staff in the office premises over the decades.

The absence of clock in and clock out norms has challenged the conventional thinking of many human resource managers who believe that employees can only be managed and controlled if they are in sight, meaning in front of their boss's eyes.

The current reality of working from home is not only demonstrated through its challenges but also its advantages to multiple stakeholders, such as employees, employers, and society. Some employers claimed mandated working from home helped them to see workers could be just as productive, or even more, outside a traditional office setting, aided by better communication tools and other technologies that have made it easier to get work done from home.

Explaining further the advantages of working from home to employer, it means happier workforces, higher retention rate, and reduced real estate footprint and office expenses. The greatest advantage is the ability to attract new talents who live in places they would not have hired in the past. This gives the employer competitive edge over rivals who insist on in-office workers.

Similarly, the benefits for employees are clear—for instance, more time with family members, go closer to extended family, and greater freedom to set and manage one's own schedule and without having to comply with official duty roster. Quoting financial service companies' real experience among claim processing staff, they found that some staff who work from home are dramatically more productive from six to ten in the morning.

On the other hand, some are more productive from one to five in the afternoon, while others are more productive in the middle of the night. Obviously, work from home allows employees to adjust their work habit at the most productive way. Highlighting sales staff who are working from home, they have more sales interaction with customers and reduced traveling time. This allows them to do a lot of prospecting, which generates more sales performance. The work from home demonstrated that some employees have greater capacity to adapt more quickly with this new place of working. They could adjust themselves in a matter of weeks.

The success of working from home, however, is strongly supported through digital technology. Digital technology's role as enabler seems like the right choice to realize work from home. Thus, every employee needs to customize its application.

Working from home during the COVID-19 pandemic lockdown has pushed employees to settle their works using multiple digital technologies, such as instant messaging, artificial intelligence, Zoom conferencing, webinar, WeChat, and Google Meet. While the home office might be here to stay, doing a work solely around a physical space is no longer a viable option.

The future of working from home is still uncertain. Working from home, which was originally intended to be a temporary measure for millions of employees in the early days of COVID-19, after more than one year of its implementation, has no clear end in sight. This scenario has led to many puzzles not only among the scholars and researchers but also among the HR managers and practitioners.

Among the questions posed are, Is working from home going to be permanent? Is office work going to end, or will employees go back to offices? Some pandemic experts are of the opinion that until social distancing guidance ends, offices cannot work at full steam. Elaborating further, office will only be open phase by phase. Another group of experts claimed the average office can work with 25–60 percent of its staff while maintaining a two-meter distance between employees.

With regard to employee reactions after COVID-19 lockdown has eased, they have mixed feelings. While some are dreaming return to the office, some are dreading. On the other hand, while some male employees are looking forward to return to office after getting tired of being at home, some female employees are still in a confused state.

The current scenario of working during the COVID-19 pandemic lockdown has *reshaped the future landscape of works*. One thing for sure is that future work designs have to consider physical contact as a critical health measure. Therefore, physical contact should be the main agenda in deciding whether the jobholder of the occupation should continue to work from home or not.

In deciding which occupation requires to work from home after the pandemic is over, it should be based on three characters: physical closeness to others, frequency of interaction, and exposure to strangers. While physical closeness to others describes how close a jobholder is required to get to other people, frequency of interaction describes how frequently a jobholder physically interacts with the same or different people. On the other hand, exposure to strangers describes how frequently a jobholder must interact with strangers.

It is quite certain that jobholders who are in the occupation of medical care, personal care, on-site customer interaction, and leisure and travel who have high physical closeness, high frequency of interaction, and high exposure to strangers have to continue to work from home for at least two to five days per week. They also have to continue applying the hybrid work platform, such as the artificial intelligence automation and robotic technology that's been used during COVID-19 pandemic lockdown.

Quoting a few example of employees who will continue to use hybrid technology platform, it includes such as online doctors and online nurses who will apply telehealth, telemedicine, video appointment and medical drown. Some health professionals predicted the application of telehealth, telemedicine, video appointment and drown will continue to rise even after the pandemic is over, which allows doctors and nurse to work from home.

Similarly, occupation in e-commerce activities—such as in the food delivery business, which hires a lot of retail and service workers—will continue to work from home. This is also due to the fact that food deliver business will be easily operated from home using e-commerce, with less physical contact, even after the pandemic. Online learning through the Zoom application, webinar, and Google meeting is expected to boom after the COVID-19 pandemic lockdown is over, which would allow teachers, lecturers, and trainers to continue work from home.

Chapter 2

COVID-19—Disease Trajectory, Virus Characteristics, and Prevention Strategies

Historically, many types of pandemic outbreaks have affected human beings throughout the years. Tracing back several pandemics that happened over the last one hundred years until the year 2000, it includes cholera, Russian influenza, the Great Plague, the Justinian plague, the Black Death, the third plague pandemic, Spanish flu, Asian flu, HIV/AIDS, and dengue. Subsequently from the year 2000 onward, several new pandemics were discovered, such as avian flu, severe acute respiratory syndrome (SARS, 2002), swine flu (2003), Middle East respiratory syndrome (MERS, 2012), Ebola (2014), Zika (2015), and recently, coronavirus '19, which is popularly known as COVID-19.

Etymologically, the term *coronavirus* originated from a Latin word that refers to *halo* or *crown* viruses, which have spikelike projection on its surface. The genome size of the virus ranges from 26 to 32×10^3 bp and consists of multiple open reading frames from six to eleven. The first open reading frames constituting 67 percent of the whole virus genome is responsible for sixteen nonstructural proteins. On the other hand, the four main structural proteins of the virus include the spike surface glycoprotein, envelope, membrane, and nucleocapsid.

Highlighting the first infections of coronavirus, it was isolated from birds with bronchitis in the 1930s. Generally, coronavirus comprises of four genera: alpha-, beta-, gamma-, and deltacoronavirus. The first two genera of coronavirus are known to infect humans, while the latter two predominantly infect birds.

Elaborating further on coronavirus that infects human, it was first discovered in the 1960s from the cultures of a patient with a common cold. This virus is responsible for almost 30 percent of common colds, and often the individuals are infected with these viruses in their lifetime. Highlighting its mutation, coronavirus infection will increase in terms of number of cases during winter and early spring.

The seriousness to study coronavirus, however, started after the severe acute respiratory syndrome (SARS) pandemic in the year 2003 and then followed by the Middle East respiratory system (MERS) pandemic in the year 2012. Scientifically, the SARS coronavirus pandemic was investigated to spread to humans through handling and consuming raccoon dogs, palm civets, and Chinese ferret-badgers sold and slaughtered at the wet markets of China. The virus-infected individuals with severe pulmonary syndrome had the mortality rate of 10 percent. Statistically, severe acute respiratory syndrome (SARS) coronavirus pandemic has affected almost 8,096 and claimed 774 lives in four continents before its containment.

Subsequent to severe acute respiratory syndrome (SARS) coronavirus, another highly pathogenic coronavirus was Middle East respiratory syndrome (MERS), which mostly affected the Arabian Peninsula. MERS coronavirus, however, lasted for seven years even after its spread in the confined area. Statistically, this coronavirus has affected 2,500 cases with a mortality rate of 35 percent.

The most severe coronavirus, however, is coronavirus '19, which is popularly known as COVID-19. Categorically, COVID-19 is considered the third major outbreak of a novel coronavirus in the new millennium after SARS and MERS. Explaining medically on the specific characteristics of the COVID-19 virus, it is *genetically similar* to the severe acute respiratory syndrome (SARS). They are also dispersed among bats, livestock, mice, humans, and other wild animals. COVID-19 also belongs to a group of betacoronavirus that is capable of infecting mammals. It is also known as animal flu or *zoonotic* in medical terms, and the most obvious behavior is that it has affected a considerable population within a short period of time. Thus, it has rapid potential to spread.

In addition, it has caused fever, cough, and shortness of breath. The most traumatizing consequence of this virus is it's known to reach and infect different parts of the human body—such as brain, nerve system, kidney, liver, gastrointestinal system—therefore causing multiple organ failure. The worst scenario is it has the potential to cause life-threatening respiratory failure.

Originated from Wuhan City, Hubei Province, China, in December 2019, the severity of COVID-19 took entire China by storm and transcended international borders in no time and reached worldwide. As a result, Wuhan City suddenly became a center of the pandemic where the first case of COVID-19 pneumonia was reported officially. In its release, the Wuhan Municipal Health Commission claimed there were twenty-seven positive COVID-19 cases found in the Southern China Animal and Seafood Wholesale Market in Wuhan. The first index cases of COVID-19 were either proprietors of the shops or individuals who had visited the market. This first trajectory was stated in an article entitled "A Novel Coronavirus Genome Identified in a Cluster of Pneumonia Cases—Wuhan, China 2019–2020."

Triggered by the Wuhan incident in December 2019, the COVID-19 virus has penetrated several countries, such as Japan, South Korea, Europe, and the United States. This uncontrolled epidemiological trend of a snowballing incident coupled with exponential growth has prompted the World Health Organization (WHO) to declare the COVID-19 outbreak as a public health emergency of international concern (PHEIC) on January 13, 2020. The worst scenario was when the World Health Organization (WHO) declared COVID-19 as a pandemic on March 11, 2020.

Subsequently, World Health Organization Situation Report-94 released that as of April 23, 2020, there were 2,544,792 confirmed cases and 175,694 deaths in two hundred countries around the globe. Ever since, the entire world has been caught off guard by the unsuspecting increase in the number of new cases due to the exponential increase in the rate of transmission. Indeed, this pandemic poses a great challenge and has caused a wave of panic.

The motivation to investigate the reasons on this rapid transmission has prompted many medical scholars, researchers, and epidemiologists in the literature.

Broadly, environmental factors, population density, inadequate sanitation, high level of mobility, and poverty on the ecosystem have vastly increased the possibility of infectious diseases, which contribute to the spread of the pandemics in recent times. Indeed, this situation has reached to an extreme point that we human beings are now our own enemies.

In addition, global warming, climate change, and reduction of agricultural lands due to population growth are among the most prominent factors. These factors have ultimately reduced or eliminated wildlife and avian habitats and increased opportunities for them to come into contact with livestock and humans. Subsequently, the coronavirus is transmitted from wildlife and birds to livestock and humans, promoting COVID-19 diseases.

Investigating at a deeper level, epidemiologists discovered several causes such as low relative humidity and low temperature, respiratory droplets of close contact with COVID-19 patient, changes in the airborne pollutant particulate, and tobacco smoking.

With regard to low relative humidity and temperature, a study reveals that COVID-19 is more stable and feasible for a longer period on smooth surface at temperatures of twenty-two to twenty-five degree Celsius and relative humidity of 40–50 percent, which suggests rapid transmission to human body. On the other hand, COVID-19 viability was rapidly lost on a shorter period at higher temperature, such as thirty-eight degree Celsius, and high relative humidity, such as more than 90 percent, which suggests slow transmission to human body.

The rapid spread of COVID-19 is also due to respiratory droplets of close contact. Epidemiologists categorized close contact into two categories: *index cases* and *traced closed contact*. A chain effect of closed contact is discovered to have accelerated the spread of the COVID-19 pandemic. In addition to close contact, changes in the airborne pollution particulate matter is also responsible in spreading the transmission of COVID-19. *Particulate matters* are hazardous solid and liquid particles, such as dust, pollen, soot, smoke, and liquid droplet suspended in air.

Similarly, tobacco smoking is also discovered to be a trigger to the spread of COVID-19. Detailing further, tobacco smoking is the single most evident activity that exposes humans to very high concentration of particulate matter in a short period of time. In addition, the damaging effect of passive smoking due to inadvertent exposure to particulate matter is also a contributing factor in spreading the diseases.

Quoting USA experience, lower bans on smoking and a higher percentage of smoking population had increased incidence of COVID-19 infection rate. Tobacco usage can be a potential risk factor not only in getting the COVID-19 viral infection but also its severe manifestations. Preexisting *comorbidities* on tobacco smokers—such as cardiovascular diseases, diabetes, respiratory diseases, and hypertension—were found to further accelerate the infection potential of COVID-19, making the treatment more challenging due to their rapid clinical deterioration.

Explaining further on mode of transmission, COVID-19 can also be easily moved across species. The major component of coronavirus transmission is the *spike glycoprotein S1* that firmly binds to *angiotensin-converting enzyme 2* (ACE2) receptor and enters the host cell. Thus, coronavirus gateway mainly depends on airways areas.

Subsequently, other means of COVID-19 spread include handshaking with infected person, contact with object or surface containing virus, repeated touching of the face (eyes, nose, or mouth), or exposure to infected patient. Recent confirmed transmission is *hidden transmission,* which is defined as unintentional spread of COVID-19 by asymptomatic virus carriers to close contacts.

With regard to exact risk population that gets infected of COVID-19, it is not yet established; however, generally it depends on demographic profiles, such as sex and age of the population. Other risk population includes those who are having more than one illness or *comorbidity*.

With regard to sex, males were found easily infected than females in both severe and nonsevere cases. In addition, males have 2.41 times more risk to develop COVID-19 infection compared to females.

With regard to age, those who fall in the age category of more than fifty years old develop 3.36 times more risk compared to those below fifty years old. The level of COVID-19 severity is even worst for those aged more than sixty-five years old, where this category of age has 0.79 times more risk compared to those below sixty-five years old.

In addition, those populations who are having more than one illness or what is called *comorbidity* in medical terms are more prone to COVID-19 than those who have no illness. The most common *comorbidity* associated with COVID-19 includes hypertension, diabetes, cardiovascular disease, respiratory disease, malignancy chronic kidney disease, and chronic liver disease. Elaborating further, those who have hypertension are more prone to COVID-19, followed by diabetes mellitus and cardiovascular.

Highlighting prevention strategies of COVID-19, it includes both pharmaceutical health initiatives and nonpharmaceutical health initiatives. While pharmaceutical health initiatives require vaccines, which is still evolving, the nonpharmaceutical health initiatives are therefore suggested by the World Health Organization.

Broadly, the major part of nonpharmaceutical public health intervention includes knowledge, attitude, and behavioral practice. It is built from various components: social distancing, wearing a mask, isolation, self-quarantine, mandated quarantine, practicing high-level self-hygiene, and increasing testing capacity.

Highlighting knowledge, attitude, and behavioral practice, it is the most profound measure to control transmission of diseases and flatten the curve of COVID-19. Attitudes are product of knowledge, and levels of attitude and knowledge are the determinants of preventive behavioral practices related to COVID-19.

Highlighting attitudes toward COVID-19, it is built from three domains: COVID-19 is a human-made disease, death is definite for those positive of COVID-19, and COVID-19 is a punishment from the Creator.

On the other hand, the domain of knowledge includes knowledge about symptoms of COVID-19, knowledge about treatment and vaccine of COVID-19, and knowledge about transmission, prevention, and incubation period of COVID-19.

Finally, preventive behavioral practice domains includes washing hands for twenty seconds, maintaining at least one-meter distance from others while outside, and avoiding crowded places.

Elaborating further on knowledge about transmission, it includes knowledge of COVID-19 behavior and ecosystem health, which are keys to controlling the spread of diseases early on their onset. Thus, expanding the knowledge on *reservoir host* of COVID-19 is an urgent and critical need to understand the nature of the pandemic.

Underpinning further knowledge about prevention, it includes maintaining social distancing, avoiding mass gatherings, washing hands with soap, and avoiding touching of mouth, nose, and eyes with unwashed hands. It also includes wearing personal protective equipment, disinfecting, cleaning, increasing testing capacity, mandated quarantining, and self-quarantining.

However, knowledge pertaining to isolation, quarantine, and community-based containment, such as social distancing, are among the major prevention knowledge suggested in the literature by epidemiologist scholars. Highlighting isolation, it is another nonpharmaceutical public health intervention carried out to safeguard the transmission of COVID-19. It is the separation of ill persons with contagious diseases from noninfected persons to protect noninfected persons; this usually occurs in hospital settings. A negative pressure could be equipped in isolation rooms to reduce transmission through aerosols.

However, since COVID-19 droplets are very large, control can be achieved without negative pressure room. Isolation of patient is particularly effective in avoiding the transmission only if early detection is possible before overt viral shedding. The isolation intervention, however, becomes too late or less effective to control the disease if the patient already transmits the COVID-19 before clinical trial.

In addition to isolation, quarantine is another effective measure used to control the transmission of COVID-19. Quarantine is manifested as movement restriction of persons who are presumed to have been exposed to a contagious disease but are not ill—either because they did not become infected or because they are still in the incubation period. Quarantine may be applied at individual level or group level and normally involves restriction to the home or designated facility. It also can be implemented voluntarily or mandatorily.

Highlighting further, it is one of the classical and most effective tools of controlling the COVID-19 pandemic. This public health measure was used widely in Italy during the fourteenth century when a ship arriving at the Venice port from plague-infected ports had to anchor and wait for forty days before disembarking their surviving passengers. Forty days of quarantine provided ample time to be completed so that asymptomatic cases could become symptomatic and therefore be identified.

During the quarantine period, all individuals should be monitored for the occurrence of any symptoms; and if such symptoms occur, they must be immediately isolated in a designated center. The reason is to treat their respiratory illness. There are several advantages of quarantine: the detection of cases is prompt and contact can be listed and traced within a short period of time.

If isolation and quarantine measures are deemed to be insufficient, community-wide containment, such as social distancing, can be implemented. Highlighting social distancing, it is *designed to reduce interactions* between people in a broader community so individuals may not be infected. Since diseases are transmitted through respiratory droplets, it requires a certain proximity of people, such as one meter. Social distancing is particularly useful in a setting where community transmission is believed to have occurred.

Many mechanisms have been implemented to realize social distancing in the society. Among the mechanisms are closure of schools or office buildings, suspension of public markets, cancellation of gatherings, closure of amusement and entertainment parks, and working from home. If social distancing measures are deemed to be insufficient, a more strict containment can be implemented

With regard to Malaysia, the government has imposed the movement control order, conditional movement control order, enhanced movement control order, and recovery movement control order to impose social distancing among the individuals in the community. While the movement control order is more rigorous, which restricts individuals to travel across the state and district borders, conditional movement control order is more relaxed, which allows individuals to travel across the state and district borders.

On the other hand, if a large number of positive cases is concentrated on a certain locality, the area will be gazetted as enhanced movement control zone. Enhanced movement control order restricts inside individuals to leave the area and outside individuals to enter the area. Conclusively, as the world awaits a medical solution, particularly a vaccine, the most effective remedy has been behavioral or nonpharmaceutical public health interventions.

Chapter 3

Global Reactions to COVID-19 Pandemic—Are They in the Same Boat?

Global approaches toward COVID-19 pandemic control, however, range from strict lockdown to minimal restriction. While some governments were quick to respond, others were not. Similarly, while some countries took extreme measures, others were lax. Countries that were quick to respond and took extreme measures include Africa, South Korea, China, Germany, New Zealand, and Malaysia. These are the countries that have science-informed leadership quality and comprehensive antipandemic arsenal.

Elaborating further on science-informed leadership quality countries, these countries are sensible to public health measures, such as having an initiative to squash the COVID-19 outbreak from the beginning. They maintained low number of infections and deaths through early decisive lockdown, implementing the surveillance systems, enforced mandated mask use, mandated social distancing, hospital quarantine, home quarantine, and targeted testing strategies. In addition, these countries used information technology through multiple applications to retrieve the affected population and geographical areas.

On the other hand, comprehensive antipandemic arsenal includes rapid establishment of disaster management team, swift scale-up in COVID-19 testing, timely reallocation of diverse resources, meticulous contact tracing to prevent asymptomatic community transmission, early cluster detection, nucleic acid testing, and home-brewed COVID-19 RT-PCR test.

Quoting Germany experience in facing the pandemic, it is among the European countries who did very well in managing the catastrophe. The most profound action that Germany took to combat the pandemic was while most politicians around the globe implemented lockdown when TV images proof that the *migrated virus* was already in the country, cases in Germany were found through indigenous virus in laboratory testing. As a result, the COVID-19 virus was detected earlier rather than during patient admission to ICU.

Germany also went into lockdown three weeks earlier compared to other countries, which is relative to the accumulation of the cases. The lockdown in Germany was short and involved rather mild intervention. Interestingly, upon lifting the lockdown measures, no new positive COVID-19 cases were reported for almost four months, which speculates that transmission might have fallen below threshold value. Evidently, this situation put Germany in favorable conditions compared to other European countries.

With regard to Malaysia, the first case was recorded on January 24, 2020; and up until March 2020, case numbers remained relatively low and occurred mainly among foreign arrivals from China. However, Malaysia had its first large daily spike on March 15, 2020, with 190 cases, in which most of them were linked to a massive religious event in Kuala Lumpur. On the following day, March 16, 2020, the cumulative case had surpassed the five hundredth mark, with the first COVID-19 death reported on March 17, 2020.

Due to rapid increase in positive cases, Malaysian government had imposed movement control order (MCO), conditional movement control order (CMCO), and enhanced movement control order (EMCO) particularly at red zone areas. All the movement control measures were carried out through mobilization of police, army, and fire personnel.

In contrast, several countries were found slow to respond to the COVID-19 pandemic, such as the US, Italy, Spain, Brazil, India, Sweden, and the UK. Explaining further on the US case study in handling COVID-19, the government lacked leadership and a unified plan to contain the pandemic, which skyrocketed daily death toll and catastrophic explosion. Similarly, there was no national lockdown plan in the US, masks were politicized, testing was discouraged for fear of rising numbers, there was worsening personal protection equipment shortages, and the most serious thing was growing distrust in science over politics.

Similarly, in Brazil, the prevention and treatment of the pandemic have also been obliterated by politics. The saddest thing is that they don't have faith in science and took a divisive role in ignoring and contradicting scientific knowledge. For instance, they sensor epidemiological data on high prevalence among indigenous people, promote hydroxychloroquine, oppose face mask and social distancing, discontinued the funding for pandemic studies, and the worst thing, opined that vaccination is not compulsory.

With regard to Italy, in the initial stage of the epidemic, the country was faced with a lack of strategic plan in confronting the catastrophe, such as dramatic shortage of protective and diagnostic equipment. All these equipment had to be imported from abroad with enormous difficulty, as each country, during that terrible moment, tried to secure its own stock. In addition, Italy also was facing other criticalities, such as neglected local medical care, unacceptable shortage of health workers, and lack of adequate infrastructure and technology.

Not only that, the most damaging situation in Italy was that there was no coordination among scientists, politicians, and societies. Although scientists had anticipated the pandemic was coming and had been saying it for years, the message never reached politicians. This mistake should not be repeated. While scientists have a task of providing politicians with all the necessary data, politicians must take responsibility to secure public health.

In addition to pharmaceutical actions, countries around the globe also reacted to the pandemic through nonpharmaceutical actions, such as by announcing multiple economic stimulus packages. Obviously, government intervention through stimulus packages has cushioned the spread of COVID-19.

Subsequent to global stimulus package initiatives with the intention to curb stock market crash due to COVID-19 perils, countries *poured down* trillions of dollars to save their livelihood and economy. Among the major measures include fiscal and monetary policy targeting households, health care, and manufacturing and servicing industries.

With regard to monetary policy, it includes liquidity support to banks and moratorium support to households. Fiscal support, on the other hand, includes allocation to household and business entities, such as small and medium enterprises, unemployment subsidy to those who lost their jobs, and employment subsidy to employers to bear the payroll cost.

South Korea, for instance, announced cash transfer to isolated persons, consumption tokens for low-income families, and income and rental support for small and medium enterprises. On the other hand, Germany enlarged entrance to temporary subsidy, improved childcare welfares for low-income parentages, and delivered grants to small and medium enterprises that were affected by the pandemic. Similarly, UK delivered much funding for their National Health Service, assisted business operations, directed donations for small businesses, reimbursed sick pay leave to affected employees, and fortified the social safety net to assist disabled individuals.

With regard to Malaysia, the government has announced three economic stimulus packages during the beginning of the pandemic with a total value of RM260 billion (USD60 billion), representing 17 percent of government GDP. It mainly comprises loan deferments, loan guarantees, one-off cash assistance, and credit facilities and rebates, as well as direct fiscal injection of Malaysian ringgit of 35 billion (USD8 billion).

Chapter 4

Implications, Challenges, and Advantages during COVID-19 Pandemic Lockdown

Broadly, the COVID-19 pandemic lockdown has brought a lot of negative energies through a life course lens. Contrarily, there are also some positive vibes that emerged unexpectedly during the pandemic lockdown. Explaining through the lens of negative implications, the COVID-19 pandemic has hastened the collapse of modern world empire, which we never imagined before. It happened during the era of globalization and advancement in science, medicine, and technology. Indeed, it has demonstrated tragic impacts to the whole world system. The COVID-19 pandemic reminded us of what we forgot, such as how we take for granted all that we have and enjoyed throughout our lifetime.

Broadly, the things that we take for granted include a healthy life, our livelihood, our freedom to travel, and our freedom to engage with societies and nations. The long arc of the twentieth century brought extraordinary gains to us, particularly our freedom to choose and predict through a life course lens. In addition, the stability and prosperity that we enjoyed after the Second World War are gone into the drain.

Obviously, the COVID-19 tragedy has changed all normal life into new normal life through its implication on multiple domains, such as unanticipated loss of human lives, unquantifiable risks to physical health, mental suffering, and exposure to world economic perils. No doubt, the COVID-19 pandemic lockdown has damaged the whole world system; however, its positive implication on the environment could not be denied, such as improvement in air quality, reduction in noise disruption, cleanliness of beaches, and low recorded carbon dioxide emission.

The most tragic implication of COVID-19, however, is the loss of human lives. Based on recent Johns Hopkins University maps and trend report (JHU, 2020), this pandemic has claimed eight hundred thousand lives globally as of May 15, 2020; while WHO (2020) reported that as of May 15, 2020, there were 4,338,658 confirmed new cases in two hundred countries.

With regard to USA alone, Johns Hopkins University data on January 19, 2021, reported 399,003 casualties coupled with 24.08 million new cases. In a similar vein, an article that appeared in MedPage Today reported the death toll in the US passes four hundred thousand, which coincides with the last of President Trump in office.

Tracing back the mortality trajectory, the first death case was reported in Wuhan on November 17, 2019, of a fifty-five-year-old man. World society is claiming that China is solely responsible for the current problem due to their negligent behavior toward social responsibility and hiding the facts related to this disease for a long period of time and not providing information to other countries in time.

With regard to unquantifiable risk to physical health, epidemiologists estimated the COVID-19 virus effects vary due to differences in testing and tracing systems. Although a large percentage of the population may eventually be infected, only a small number become ill, require hospitalization, need intensive care treatment, and die. No doubt, knowledge about short-term course of individual infections and effective treatment is improving, but there is still much to learn about long-term physical health risks.

Broadly, the physical health risks of the virus increase strikingly by patients' age and patients having more than one preexisting illness and are greater for men. The risk is also high for migrant groups, which are intertwined with social disadvantage. Exposure, infection, and quality of physical health care are directly and indirectly related to occupations and standard of living condition, and the implication is more severe especially for societies without universal health care.

Those frontliners who are in the field of health, safety, food, and transport are more prone to this virus. Similarly, people who stay in high-poverty neighborhood, such as squatters with high population density and cramped areas, are directly exposed to this virus. High-stress-job employees, such as those who are working in the gig economy sector, also have greater risk because of their weakening immune system.

In addition to physical health deterioration, lockdown, quarantine, isolation, and social distancing, the COVID-19 pandemic has greatly reduced social contacts with a consequent increase of mental suffering challenges and psychological-related diseases. The phenomenon is proven based on several studies that COVID-19 pandemic is not only compromising physical health but also increasing mental-related suffering.

However, the types and severity of mental suffering due to COVID-19 may vary among people with different health conditions, ages, social roles, occupation, and lifestyle. Thus, the mental health status of the population during the pandemic is of great importance. Mental suffering problems have occurred among frontliners in the health industry during the outbreak. Underpinning further on health care workers, the mental suffering of dealing with COVID-19 patients could reduce ability to perform their job and even lead to lack of clinical competency.

Broadly, the COVID-19 pandemic has heightened multiple types of mental suffering, beginning from depression to fear, acute stress, loneliness, insomnia disorder, and post-traumatic stress disorder; and the most serious implication is it triggers particularly COVID-19 patients to suicidal thoughts and attempts.

With regard to depression, fear, and acute stress, it is the outcome of COVID-19 experience. It is predicted that an individual with exposure to COVID-19 would be more depressed and would fear about getting sick from the virus than those without any COVID-19 exposure.

Although social distancing is considered a key mechanism in the global effort to slow the spread of COVID-19, it could lead to other mental illness, such as a feeling of social isolation and exacerbated loneliness particularly among aging generation. This is due to the fact that older adults are particularly vulnerable, as they are less likely to engage online and more susceptible to COVID-19.

Contrarily, loneliness could also affect people at all ages during the pandemic. Explaining further on how serious the feeling of loneliness during isolation and quarantine is, several psychologists discovered it is incredibly detrimental to mental health, as it could cause early mortality—meaning those who are chronically lonely are more likely to die early. In a worst scenario, loneliness during pandemic is dangerous since it can cause hypervigilance regarding social threats.

Subsequent to multiple chains of depression, fear, acute stress, and loneliness outcomes due to COVID-19, it could trigger a more serious mental illness, such as insomnia disorder. Clinically, insomnia disorder is discovered as one of the major psychiatric disorders among COVID-19 patients and survivors. The main manifestations of insomnia disorder include perceived sleep dissatisfaction and difficulty in initiating or maintaining sleep, which lead to cognitive impairment, mood disturbances, and fatigue during the COVID-19 pandemic lockdown. Obviously, insomnia seems to be affecting more people during the COVID-19 pandemic.

Having all the mental illnesses above, it could lead to post-traumatic stress disorder among COVID-19 survivors. Post-traumatic stress disorder is defined as development of symptoms related to avoidance, negative alterations in mood and cognition, intrusion, reactivity, and arousal following exposure to COVID-19 traumatic event. Generally, there are three significant disturbances faced by COVID-19 survivors: near-death experience, confusion, and ICU-related trauma.

Detailing near-death experience further, patients with severe COVID-19 may have experienced respiratory difficulties that could advance to respiratory failure. Therefore, while treatment is given, it may involve extra burden on them, such as limited ability to communicate, feeling of loss of control, and pain from medical interventions such as endotracheal intubation. Other near-to-death experience faced by severe COVID-19 patients is confusion during the treatment. COVID-19 patients also may face several ICU-related trauma such as feelings of guilt, mood swings, and memories of panic and suffocation.

Finally, the greatest mental risk experienced during COVID-19 is suicidal behavior, which includes suicidal thought, suicidal attempt, and murder-suicide. The issue on suicidal behavior during the lockdown is alarming. The linkages between COVID-19 and suicidal ideation unveiled potential increases in suicidal thinking since the beginning of the COVID-19 pandemic.

The suicidal behavioral decisions, however, do not happen in a vacuum. There are multiple mental suffering factors that could lead to suicidal thought, suicidal attempt, or murder-suicide. Among the factors are depression, stress, loneliness, decreased access to community and religious support, barriers to mental health treatment, widespread anxiety, and medical problems.

Explaining on livelihood, the COVID-19 pandemic has exposed the world population to many economic perils and disasters. The uniqueness of COVID-19, compared to previous pandemics, is its knockdown effects have strongly damaged the whole economic infrastructure, which has never happened before in the history of mankind. Strengthening further on its severity, the economic perils due to COVID-19 have substantial negative and nonsensual impact on many stakeholders, such as governments, suppliers, employees, businessmen, and individuals.

Broadly, there are many economic perils on human livelihood due to the COVID-19 pandemic. However, the most serious perils are varying from economic slowdown to poor performance of stock exchange, disruption of supply chain flow, collapse of tourism and hospitality industries, and increased rate of poverty level; and the most traumatic effect is losing a job.

Highlighting economic slowdown, a report from International Monetary Fund (2020) revealed that all economies—including developed, emerging, and even developing—will likely experience recession. Strengthening further on the recession statistics, IMF (2020) projected 8 percent of global recession. In a similar vein, International Monetary Fund's April 2020 World Outlook projected a drop of 3 percent for the world economy. This projected drop is extremely high compared to the world financial crisis in 2009, which was only 0.1 percent. Thus, these results indicate that the wave of consequences of COVID-19 is still extending. Its effect is not yet over.

Many countries experience losses due to *suppression* of economic activities. Economies in the advanced countries are expected to shrink by minus 6.1 percent, while recession in emerging and developing economies is projected to be less adverse compared to developed nations. However, China and India are expected to record positive growth by the end of 2020. All in all, IMF (2020) predicted that the cumulative loss over the year 2021 from COVID-19 is about US$9 trillion.

Subsequent to economic slowdown, COVID-19 also has brought poor performance of global stock exchange. COVID-19 has destructed the market volatility and brought shock to the stock market. The profound reason on why stock exchange through market volatility reacted heavily to COVID-19 is due to the government restrictions on many commercial activities through mandated social distancing and lockdown.

Similarly, through mandated social distancing and lockdown, COVID-19 also damaged the operation of global supply chain, a critical pulse that connects a large number of manufacturers with foreign firms for their raw material. Explaining further, the COVID-19 outbreak has caused a disastrous crisis, such as disruption of supply chain from foreign firms to manufacturers, which subsequently forces the manufacturers to shut down their operation, merely to prevent the spread of the infection.

Among the supply chain disruption includes how manufacturing industries cannot start production, which subsequently affects the upstream and downstream enterprises. The supply chain disruption is getting even worse due to the reduction, delay, and postponement of flights during the pandemic lockdown.

In a similar vein, supply chain disruption has resulted in the reduction of market demand for goods and services particularly in exporting and importing companies. While exporting countries faced lack of output for their local firms, importing countries faced unavailability of raw materials. Some experts and professionals anticipated that the COVID-19 pandemic, which damaged the whole infrastructure of global supply chains, has the possibility to create cross-border economic disaster at a high-scale level.

Compared to several previous pandemics—such as SARS, MERS, and Spanish flu—the invisible COVID-19 outbreak effect on global supply chain is far reaching with large catastrophic consequences. It is also worth noting that occurrence of disruption in the supply chains resulted in a decrease of business performance. This situation has prompted many manufacturers observing on the importance of handling the disruption effectively and successfully at each stage of the global chains.

Quoting China's traumatic experience in facing supply chain disruption during the COVID-19 pandemic lockdown, millions of supplies are stuck in China since the postponement and cancellation of sea freights. The scenario is even worst knowing that China is a world factory that produces one-third of the production for many countries.

Citing several impacted industries, for instance, the entire world's pharmaceutical manufacturers are heavily reliant on China for their raw materials. Similarly, China also produces a large amount of world's intermittent parts for the creation of personal computer, mobile phone supply, global television parts, and textile. Since majority of this raw material production are going to other countries, a shock in the production due to supply disruption will severely affect global supply chain infrastructure during the pandemic lockdown.

With regard to sectoral analysis, the tourism and hospitality sector is among the most fragile sectors that were greatly affected during the COVID-19 pandemic lockdown. No doubt, the sector used to be affected by various crises and outbreaks before—such as terrorism, earthquake, Ebola, SARS, and Zika—but the nature, the unprecedented circumstances, and the impact of COVID-19 demonstrate signs that this outbreak is unique and different. This is due to the fact that COVID-19 has profound and long-lasting structural and transformational effect on travelers' socioeconomic behaviors and market, which could lead to the collapse of the industry.

Explaining this scenario further, it is expected that international tourist arrivals will drop, causing million-dollar losses of export revenues. With regard to staff layoff, COVID-19 has caused millions of direct tourism job cuts, representing seven times the impact of the September 11 crisis, the largest decline in history.

Discussing further, the implication of COVID-19 on the tourism industry can be viewed from two perspectives: tourism demand and tourism supply. While tourism demand is focused on tourists' bad and traumatic experiences during the lockdown, tourism supply is focused on tourist operators' stressful experience in handling tourist journey.

With regard to tourism demand, COVID-19 has created bad experience to many tourists and holidaymakers, such as trip cancellations, loss of money paid for travel, trip disruptions, loss of travel loyalty benefits and points, travel restriction, and travel ban; and the most sickening experiences are quarantines and social distancing. On the other hand, pressure on tourism supply includes tourist operators' stressful experience in complying with the new normal of managing the safety and health of tourists and handling communication pressure with tourists.

Underpinning further on new normal of managing the safety and health of tourists during COVID-19, it includes complying with cleaning and hygiene protocol in terms of protective measures—for instance, providing masks, sanitizers, thermometer, and disinfecting wipes. In addition, tourist operators also need to manage the tourist crowd through social distancing practices and redesign the sitting layout during the journey to make it contactless. Elaborating on handling communication pressure with tourists during the COVID-19 pandemic, it includes unanticipated changes of travel itineraries and bookings, cancellation of bookings, and the worst scenario, refunding the compensation.

Conclusively, the COVID-19 pandemic lockdown taught several lessons to the tourism industry. Among the lessons include that the industry needs multiskilled employees to solve issues of reduced redundancy and retaining the employees in the future. This could be done by adding more responsibilities during job training and across the department. Secondly, the industry should prioritize hygiene and sanitation practices as mandated norms and foreseeable in every traveler's action. Thirdly, tourism and hospitality management must consider wearing masks mandatory until a sustained solution—for instance, the vaccine—is discovered.

Colossal economic loss that affected many countries during the pandemic lockdown also contributes to massive poverty. Strengthening further, millions of people could be pushed into hard-core poverty, which will deepen social inequality.

Among them are people with less-protected and low-paid jobs. Explaining further on less-protected people, the COVID-19 pandemic lockdown has led to skyrocketing poverty level among young people. Young people, those who fall under the age category between sixteen and twenty-four years old, are the most vulnerable group. This is due to the fact that they typically have short-term and seasonal employment ties, such as on contractual and temporary basis.

The COVID-19 pandemic lockdown is not only advancing the poverty level among young people but may also increase global job loss in the medium and long term among millions of people worldwide. Obviously, the effects of this crisis are greater than the global financial crisis that happened in 2008–2009. Explaining to a worst-extent implication, the job loss condition is not only expected to reduce employees' wages but also reduced take home pay which is budgeted for their spouse and children. The impact of COVID-19 on global unemployment rate of now is scary.

Highlighting COVID-19 implication on social events, COVID-19 has resulted in the disruption of daily lives, as millions are quarantined and isolated, borders are shut, schools are closed, panic buying is accumulated, and food is scarce. Many international events, social events, family events, marriages, ceremonies, and business events are being postponed or canceled.

With regard to health care workers, first responders, armed forces, fire personnel, policemen, essential service providers, and other frontliners, they have taken a direct hit. They are trying their best to fight against the deadly virus with little protective gear and falling prey to the virus at alarming rate.

Despite the many detrimental effects, COVID-19 has provoked some natural and changes in behavior and attitudes with positive influences on the environment. Among the positive effects are improvement in air quality, reduction in environmental noise, increased cleanliness of beaches and rivers, and decline in primary energy use. In addition, other positive effects include low recorded carbon dioxide emission and boost in digitalization.

The total lockdown during the COVID-19 pandemic has triggered significant reduction in air pollution from exhaust fumes, cars, power plants, and other sources of fuel combustion emissions, which allow for improvement of air quality, particularly in major cities around the globe. Geographically, major key cities in the world experienced huge reductions in air pollution.

Alongside the reduction in air pollutants during the COVID-19 pandemic lockdown is a massive reduction in environmental noise. This has contributed into positive effect in sleeping pattern, metabolism, and cognitive ability in children. Strengthening further on the positive after effect of the COVID-19 pandemic lockdown, not only has it reduced traffic congestion but it also has improved the pleasant atmosphere.

Subsequently, notable changes have also been observed on the increased cleanliness of beaches during the COVID-19 pandemic lockdown, particularly in term of its physical appearances. Beaches constitute the interface between land and ocean offering coastal protection from cyclone and marine storms. It is also an integral part of natural capital assets found in coastal areas. Generally, beaches provide services such as tourism and recreation that are crucial in the economic well-being of countries.

With regard to primary energy consumption, the demand for energy reduced during the pandemic lockdown. Thus, this result revealed another positive effect of COVID-19. The massive reduction in energy demand triggered by the COVID-19 pandemic lockdown also accounted for the dramatic decline in global carbon dioxide emissions. Strengthening further, the annual carbon dioxide emission has not only been anticipated to fall at a rate never seen before but the fall is also envisioned to be the biggest in the single year of 2020.

Chapter 5

Nature and Characteristics of Working from Home during Pre-COVID-19 and Post-COVID-19 Era. What Makes the Difference?

The first pre-COVID-19 work-from-home policy was adopted in 1973, when OPEC imposed embargo on oil price, which triggered the price acceleration in the market. The increase in oil prices had made commuting cost for employees more expensive and therefore pushed oil companies to change from traditional and collocated work policy to work-from-home policy, which allowed employees to work remotely.

Generally, during post-COVID-19 outbreak, employees were forced to work from home due to social distancing requirements mandated by their residence countries. It is important to note, however, that this enforced working from home was far different to any pre-COVID-19 working-from-home scenario. Firstly, during post-COVID-19, none of the employees had the choice to work from home, but rather they were forced by government regulations. Secondly, most of the employees needed to work from home, not only a few employees or teams. Thirdly, due to high infections risks and death toll, employees were concerned about their own, their families', and their work colleagues' health, which put additional stress on employees.

The difference can also be observed between old and new human resource school of thoughts on working from home during pre-COVID-19 and post-COVID-19, respectively. Obviously, for a long time during pre-COVID-19, working from home was viewed simply as a perk or luxury for special employees by human resource practitioners. Most human resource managers from the old school of thought in the 1980s were largely against the idea because they were concerned about the loss of productivity when employees would do their work from home. Those human resource mindset was yet to adjust to the fact that employees were not just spending most of the day sitting at home eating lunch and not actually working.

Strengthening further on this cynical view, human resource managers from the old school of thought claimed that employees who work from home were "actually not working." Their claim, however, stemmed from the conservative managerial mindset that fears the loss of control—for instance, the performance of employees cannot be measured if they are not in direct sight of employer.

Apparently, during the pre-COVID-19 era, the idea of working from home was in the air but not proceeding very far or fast. This is proven by viewing the trend during pre-COVID-19 where only 10 percent of the employees actually work full-time from home and 20 percent work from home at least some of the time. However, during the post-COVID-19 outbreak, almost 100 percent of the employees who could work from home did so, which totally changed the idea of working from home overnight. This dramatic change emerged about the end of March 2020 and continues until today.

With regard to number of days working from home, during pre-COVID-19, employees were required to work from home for every alternate days or alternate two days leisurely. Contrarily, during post-COVID-19, employees are mandated to work from home almost every day intensively without fail.

The uniqueness of post-COVID-19 is that it brings the largest test market in the history of human resource practices by forcing almost all organizations and entities to adopt a work-from-home policy even without sufficient written human resource policy on managing people. This inclusive approach of forced work-from-home exercise brought about a number of important and interesting outcomes that organizations have to adjust, whether they like it or not, over the next several years.

On the other hand, during pre-COVID-19, the practice of managing people through work-from-home policy is exclusive only for certain technological giant companies. Among the companies are Twitter, Square, Facebook, Google, Microsoft,

Morgan Stanley, Capital One, Zillow, Slack, Amazon, and PayPal, who had practiced the working-from-home policy during pre-COVID-19.

Viewing from planning and preparation perspective, the post-COVID-19 outbreak provided unique context in the sense that it did not allow much time for employers to plan in facing the new work condition procedure. Organizations have been caught off guard and were ill-prepared for the sudden implementation of the working-from-home policy. The implication on employee side is that they feel traumatized for the sudden changes from office-work setting to home-based setting. The trauma is further worsen when face-to-face job interaction, which has been practiced for years, has now become occupational hazard.

This scenario, however, was totally different during pre-COVID-19, where employers were well prepared to implement the work-from-home policy since it was already embedded in the organization's human resource practices. Similarly viewing from employees' perspective, they felt much pleasure and leisure working from home since the procedures were clearly articulated in the human resource job manual.

Explaining further on the characteristics of working from home between pre-COVID-19 and post-COVID-19 era, it also can be viewed from five dimensions: degree of motivation, degree of complexity in shifting from office to home, extent of digital learning acceptance behavior, changes of job across occupation, and employees' well-being.

Explaining extent of employees' motivation toward working from home, it is, however, different between the pre-COVID-19 and post-COVID-19 era. During pre-COVID-19, the intention to work from home was highly motivated. This was due to the fact that employees experienced fewer distractions, fatigue, stress, and confusion. Highlighting further, they felt more prepared and engaged toward their job, which led to their retention within the organization. On the other hand, the sudden shock of working from home during post-COVID-19 has created a lot of mental and physical sufferings to the employees, such as feeling of stress, confusion, phobia, anxiety, burnout, and fatigue.

Similarly, sudden shifting of work from office to home brings more complexity during post-COVID-19 due to unsettled office space at home compared to pre-COVID-19 where the office was already built-in within the home environment. During post-COVID-19, employees face ergonomic fatigue with mock-up space, such as the kitchen or living room being converted to office space. On the other hand, during pre-COVID-19, employees enjoyed ergonomic wellness, which was characterized by ready-to-use office space equipped with desktop computer, Zoom application, virtual meeting room, and silent space that was away from children noise at home.

With regard to technology, employees who are working from home have more profound behavior in learning the digital application during pre-COVID-19 compared to post-COVID-19. During pre-COVID-19, employees had more intentions to adopt the technology due to the ample time provided to them through training. There was no element of stress, fatigue, and burnout during the learning. However, since digital technologies were forced to apply during post-COVID-19, it has invited multiple levels of mental suffering, such as fatigue, resistance, and disengagement among the employees.

The greatest challenge of working from home during post-COVID-19, however, is many employees change their job across occupation due to their inexperience to work from home. There are also certain jobs that are fully unfit to be performed from home. Quoting US experience during post-COVID-19, only some of the jobs can be done fully from home, while the rest cannot be done fully from home. This scenario has caused disappearances of some occupation and a dramatic growth in other occupation. Contrarily, this scenario did not happen during pre-COVID-19 since the job was being shared between home and office, respectively.

With regard to well-being, employees who are working from home during post-COVID-19 are exposed to multiple mental sufferings, such as anxiety, phobia, stress, burnout, reduced life satisfaction, negative news, and fear of being infected or infecting others around them. The most serious effect is that face-to-face job interaction became an occupational hazard. Contrarily, during pre-COVID-19 era, employees felt more engaged with their works and experienced a high level of job flexibility and autonomy. The summary of major differences between pre-COVID-19 working from home and post-COVID-19 working from home is shown in Table 5.1 below.

Table 5.1: The Summary of Major Differences between Pre-COVID-19 Working from Home and Post-COVID-19 Working from Home

Domain	Pre-COVID-19	Post-COVID-19
Approach	Exclusive for some employees only	Inclusive for all employees
Government interventions	No intervention from governments	Full intervention from governments
Choice	Voluntary	Enforced
Mental preparedness	Looking forward to work from home, less distraction from family members	Confused, blurred, shocked, increased anxiety, and fearful due to sudden implementation
Clarity between domain of work and home	Very clear about both domains	Not clear about both domains, mixed up between formal office work and informal home work, such as writing a proposal, giving lecture through webinar, cleaning, and cooking
Availability of work-from-home policy	The policy articulates sufficient work-from-home modus operandi.	A lot of companies do not have proper work-from-home policy.

Availability of employees' handbook on work-from-home policy	Available	Not available
Job role	High flexibility, high autonomy, and high empowerment	Confused and blurred about job role and autonomy since it is the first experience
Responsibilities	Professionally carrying out the job	Cannot act professionally due to first time doing it
Job environment	Less distraction and high privacy	A lot of distraction, especially from family members
Physical work space	Cozy and well-prepared home office with attached desktop and strong internet connectivity and have gone through training on the application of digital technology	Poor ergonomics—kitchen table converted into office table, bedroom converted into office space—poor internet connectivity, and new to digital technology
Mobility	Free to travel for business and social visits	A lot of restrictions to travel for business and social visits
Social interactions	Flexibility in face-to-face contact	Inflexibility in face-to-face contact

Chapter 6

Is Work from Home Favor to Every Task, Occupation, Sector, and Country during COVID-19 Pandemic Lockdown?

Although work from home is forced by government authority onto all employees and employers during the COVID-19 pandemic lockdown, the great question is, Is it favor to every task, occupation, sector, and country? The mandated call to work from home has created a lot of polemic, particularly among the employees and employers who never experienced it before. Furthermore, more than half of the workforce globally has little knowledge or are not ready to work from home.

Highlighting its implication on human resource practices, particularly on employees' work condition, this call has created a new landmark on employees' attendance procedures in the office premises. Over the decades, employees' attendance in the office premises have been measured and documented through punch-in and punch-out acts. However, now this punctuality behavior is no longer relevant anymore.

Based on human resource practice, the work-from-home policy is not favor to every employee and employer. The success of work-from-home policy, however, is influenced by multiple factors. Elaborating further, the success of the so-called *neo-workplace policy* is determined largely by the nature of tasks, occupation profiles, income, sector, economy, and countries.

The strongest factor that determines the potentiality of working from home is the nature of tasks. Elaborating further, task is an actual collection of activities under each category of jobholders' occupation. The location where the task is naturally being carried out, whether on the field site or off the field site, is an important criterion to justify the suitability of the work to be operated from home.

Generally, if large activities of tasks are involved on the field site, then work from home is not possible. Contrarily, if large activities of tasks are involved off the field site, then work from home is possible. Similarly, tasks that could be performed through high social distance have the potential to be operated from home. On the other hand, tasks that involve high social interaction do not favor work from home.

Broadly, there are three categories of tasks: spatial tasks, interpersonal tasks, and physical tasks. Spatial and interpersonal tasks favor work from home, while physical tasks do not favor work from home. Spatial tasks require comfortable space to perform the tasks. Among the tasks are keying in data, analyzing data, writing conceptual paper, authoring books, giving lectures, and processing claims. The spatial tasks demand for less hassle procedures, in which they could be done from home silently.

On the other hand, interpersonal tasks—such as communication with clients, convincing clients, motivating clients and suppliers, and giving feedback to client—almost could be done from home and, of course, with the help of Zoom and Google meeting applications.

Unfortunately, not all categories of tasks favor work from home. Physical tasks, for instance, require the employees to be physically present on-site to do their work. While some physical tasks require fixed equipment attach to their workstation, some do not need fixed equipment. However, their work demands them to be on field site all the time.

The physical tasks that require fixed equipment include operating machines, laboratory equipment, x-ray rooms, scanning machines, copying machines, and operating theater tools. All these categories of physical tasks could not be performed without tools, which demands employees to work away from home. Other examples of physical tasks that do not require fixed equipment but still need to operate away from home include dealing with violent people, working outdoors every day, spending majority of time walking and running, spending majority of time wearing safety equipment, and working directly with the public. The summary of the tasks that is favor and in favor to work from home is shown in Table 6.1 below.

Table 6.1: Summary of Tasks that Can Be Done from Home and Cannot Be Done from Home

Domain of Works	Tasks that Is Favor to Work from Home	Tasks that Is Not Favor to Work from Home
Assisting and caring for others	Make travel itinerary	Provide assistance during emergencies
Measuring products or surrounding	Analyzing building costs	Measure depth of construction under surface
Thinking creatively	Design layouts for print publication	Creating physical prototype
Interacting with computers	Create electronic data backup	Set up computer hardware
Processing, analyzing, and interpreting information	Analyze industry trend	Analyze crime scene evidence
Communicating and establishing interpersonal relationship	Answering client emails	Represent clients in legal proceedings
Training, teaching, coaching, and developing others	Instruct college students	Train housekeeping service personnel

Performing administrative and organizational activities	Arrange facility schedules	Operate cash register
Updating knowledge and learning	Attend online seminar	Attend surgical skills course
Selling to or influencing others	Market product, services, and events	Distribute samples
Monitoring processes, surroundings, or use of services	Monitor market trend	Patrol properties to maintain safety
Equipment, materials, and machinery	Test software performance	Inspect cargo hazards

In addition to nature of tasks, the occupation characteristic is another benchmark used to justify whether the work could be done from home or not. Generally, occupation consists of a cluster of similar job title. Occupations such as teacher, lecturer, software consultant, counselor, research analyst, data analyst, and corporate communication manager are among the occupations that have high potential to be carried out from home, although with the help of technology.

Contrarily, occupations such as production manager, production control manager, pilot, stewardess, site clerk, dispatcher, and barber are among the occupation that do not favor work from home. The characteristics of occupation that do and do not favor to work from home is shown in Table 6.2 below.

Table 6.2: Occupation Characteristics that Do and Do Not Favor to Work from Home

Occupation Characteristics	Cannot Perform from Home	Can Perform from Home
Use email less than once a month	✓	
Use email almost every day		✓
Deal with violent people at least once a month	✓	
Work outdoors every day	✓	
Work outdoors once a month		✓
Exposed to minor burns, cuts, bites, or stings at least once a week	✓	
Spend majority of time walking or running	✓	
Spend majority of time writing report, proposal, and speech		✓
Spend majority of time wearing common or specialized protective or safety equipment	✓	
Performing general physical activities is very important	✓	
Handling and moving objects is very important	✓	

Presenting business plan report every week		✓
Sending courier to customers every day	✓	
Giving lectures every day		✓
Repairing and maintaining electronic equipment is very important	✓	
Inspecting patients every day	✓	

The potentiality to work from home also depends on sectoral classification. Finance and insurance sectors have the highest potential, in which three-quarters of the time is spent on activities that can be done from home without loss of productivity. Similarly, information technology and business services and management have the next highest potential, where more than half of the employees' hour is spent on activities that could be done effectively from home.

At the extreme point, there are several sectors that totally do not support the potentiality of working from home. These include those employees who are working in the hospitality, wholesale, retail trade, transportation construction, accommodation, and agricultural sectors. The potentiality of working from home based on sectors is shown in table 6.3 below.

Table 6.3: Potential Share of Time Spent Working from Home by Sectors

Sectors	Percentages of Time Spent to Work from Home	Potentiality to Work from Home
Finance and insurance	76–86	High
Management	68–78	High
Professional, scientific, and technical services	62–75	High
IT and telecommunication	58–69	High
Education	33–69	High
Wholesale trade	41–52	High
Real estate	32–44	Moderate
Government and administrative support	31–42	Moderate
Utilities	31–37	Moderate
Art, entertainment, and recreation	19–32	Moderate
Health care and social assistance	20–29	Moderate
Retail trade	18–28	Moderate
Mining	19–25	Low
Manufacturing	19–23	Low

Transportation and warehousing	18–22	Low
Construction	15–20	Low
Accommodation and food services	8–9	Low
Agriculture	7–8	Low

Subsequently, employees in the occupation that possess high potential to work from home are also those who are from high-income bracket, highly educated, holding high-end positions, and highly talented, competent, and skillful. Contrarily, employees in the occupation that possess low potential to work from home are also those from low-income bracket, holding low-end position, lowly educated, and fall in 3D categories: dirty, difficult, and dangerous work.

Viewing from economic perspective, work from home is more potential in highly advanced economies compared to emerging and low economies. Employees in advanced economies spend more hours working from home compared to emerging economies. For instance, based on weekly basis, Britain is spending thirty-three to forty-six hours, German is spending thirty to thirty-nine hours, USA is spending twenty-nine to thirty-nine hours, Japan is spending twenty-nine to thirty-nine hours, and France is spending twenty-eight to thirty-nine hours working from home, respectively, without losing productivity. Contrarily, in emerging economies—such as Mexico, China, and India—employees are spending less hours working from home. Mexico, for instance, is spending eighteen to twenty-six hours, China is spending sixteen to twenty-two hours, and India is spending twelve to sixteen hours per week working from home.

Highlighting on poor countries, such as Latin America and Caribbean, only 7 percent of employees in Guatemala and 16 percent in Bahamas could work from home, respectively. Explaining on the percentage of hours that is feasible to be done from home in developing countries, such as Ghana, only 6 percent of the working hours can be done from the house.

Based on all these scenario, the potentiality of working from home is not meant for all employees and employers. The reality is that not all works can be done completely from home, neither from the office. While some works can be done from home, some works require on-site physical presence. Quoting the United States workforce experience, hybrid model unveiled that only 22 percent of the employees can work from home, between three and five days a week, without affecting productivity. In contrast, 61 percent of them can work no more than a few hours a week from the house, which suggests more hours at office sites. The remaining 17 percent of the workforce, however, can work from the house partially, between one and three days per week.

Chapter 7

The Challenges of Working from Home during COVID-19 Pandemic Lockdown

Generally, work from home poses many challenges for employees, employers, and societies. Explaining the worst scenario, the implementation of work from home was done haphazardly, which forced many organizations to shut their doors and send staff home. This situation is something unimaginable and has never been thought before in the history of mankind.

The sudden implementation of work from home is rather damaging, and for some employers and employees particularly, it is a nightmare, scary and stressful. Several disadvantages to employers when employees are working from home include employee turnover, difficulty to innovate their employees, loss of control of employees, and miss the opportunity to attend strategic level meeting at headquarters level.

With regard to employee turnover, this is the major disadvantage to employers allowing employees to work from home. Employees who work from home are dramatically more likely to quit than employees who routinely work in the office setting. This is due to the fact that employees who work from home lose all the important social fabric with their working colleagues, such as how they cannot go for lunch together, cannot go for happy hour, cannot go for coffee break, and miss the chance to attend corporate dinner.

In addition to employee turnover disadvantage, employers also found it difficult to innovate and collaborate with their employees. It was found difficult for employers to generate new ideas when employees are working from home rather than in office setting. The reason was because employers can have moments of serendipity when employees come together, discuss, or share ideas. This scenario can be observed when employees are batting ideas back and forth, which creates more innovation than when they work in isolation or through videoconferencing. On the employer side, this could be a subtle disadvantage until videoconferencing technology is more fully developed to enhance the critical process.

Another argument that supports disadvantage to employers is based on several old business school conventionalists who claimed that employees who work from home are "actually not working." Their claim, however, stems from the conservative managerial mindset that fears "the lost of control"—for instance, the productivity of employees cannot be measured if they are not in direct sight of employer.

In a similar vein, which explained disadvantage to employers, some employers claimed that while working from home during the pandemic lockdown, they miss an opportunity to attend major corporate decision meeting, particularly on HR issues such as promotion and compensation. As such, they feel of being alienated from the company's major decision and sometimes even promotion. Subsequent to this, they lose touch on all matters pertaining to the organization's critical issues and strategic decisions.

Similar to disadvantages to employers, working from home also brought some disadvantages to employees. Broadly, working from home has caused several unprecedented challenges to employees' working lives. Among the major challenges are distraction at home, sedentary life behavior, ergonomic challenges, loss of culture and corporate identity, and employees' experience of mental sufferings. Employees are also experiencing increase number of working hours, imbalance between work and life interplay, and technological challenges.

Highlighting distraction, employees who are working from home are susceptible to distraction because of the activities going on in the house, such as crying children, ringing doorbells, and noisy pets. Their children or spouses, for those married employees, could easily distract them even if they try to create a space in the house as a workstation. Explaining further, one specific distraction that is inevitable could create conflict at home. Their work could be distracted when conflict erupts at home. No doubt, experiencing distraction at home is a normal consequence for married couples; however, conflict with spouses is a different thing because it has lasting emotional implications on the performance of the job.

Work from home requires employees to isolate and distance themselves, which could lead to sedentary behaviors. Among the sedentary behaviors is being less physically active during the workday as compared to working from office, which required them to walk to lunch, walk to tea break, walk up and down stairs, and walk to attend meeting. Having a fewer steps while working from home could lead to multiple health risks, such as diabetes, high blood pressure, and cardiovascular problems.

Working from home also brings ergonomic challenge, where home office is becoming a permanent fixture. The greatest challenge is many households need to share same space to pursue their private, educational, and professional activities. Employees had to prepare a mock-up workspace at home—kitchen and living room—to face their work demands. Unless their dwellings were already renovated into home offices, they were forced to upgrade on the fly—for instance, couches became office chairs, kitchen table became desk, and bedroom and family hall became workspace.

In addition to ergonomic challenge, the work-from-home trend contend that companies will lose their culture and corporate identity. Newly recruited young employees, who are in the categories of generation Y and generation Z, miss the touch of social interactions. They are no longer enjoying the camaraderie at work—for instance, going out to lunch together, having a drink after work, or attending corporate dinner party. This corporate identity will definitely be missed while they are working from home.

Lack of social interaction while working from home also has put pressure on the employees. Many of the employees feel under pressure given the blurring of the line that separated their professional and personal life. While working from home, many employees are under house arrest and are experiencing multiple levels of mental suffering diseases—such as acute stress, insomnia, feeling of loneliness, anxiety, and intrusive thoughts—plagued with depression, and the worst scenario, worrying about getting COVID-19.

Highlighting specifically on job burnout—such as exhaustion, cynicism, and depersonalization—it is another emerging critical issue experienced by employees while working from home. Employees' burnout inevitably is expected to be a longer-term risk and therefore should be an utmost concern to employers. Several psychologists, however, suggested three tips to avoid burnout during working from home: maintain physical and social boundaries, maintain temporal boundaries as much as possible, and focus on the most important work. By practicing these three tips, employees' burnout may be reduced, which subsequently increases their mental health.

Quite suddenly and unexpectedly, employees who work from home face the challenges of mixing office work with housework such as sweeping, cleaning, writing a business proposal, cooking, and attending Zoom meetings. They face the challenge to draw a clear line between office work and housework. The worst scenario of working from home includes difficulty to unplug working hours, which burdens them with extra work.

Unconsciously, working from home has also increased working hours for some employees. The wholesale shift into working-from-home culture has brought shock, which forced employees to recognize, call out, and reject dangerous norms. Among the most obvious norms is the working hour fallacy that disproportionately affects employees. Employees' working hours in many countries have increased dramatically during the pandemic lockdown. Extremely surprising is how employees are starting work earlier but finishing at the same time. This is perhaps because people are not commuting and instead of sitting in traffic, they choose to work.

Highlighting the negative influence of work from home on work-life interplay, it is observed that employees who work from home suffered from increased work-to-life and life-to-work conflict. Indeed, work from home triggered greater work-related fatigue, which worsened the perceived work-life balance. Explaining further the negative side effect of work from home, it also worsened their daily leisure and pleasure activities. This is due to overlapping between private life and work, which leads to greater contamination of personal concern and work duties.

With regard to technological challenges, its application brought several deficiencies, such as how employees are not fully engaged with their works, lack of nonverbal cues in communicating, and loss of touch with work. Other challenges include cybersecurity, technological fatigue, and unreadiness to use new applications.

Quoting experience using applications such as WeChat, WhatsApp, and Facebook, the negative effect is far more complex and scary. While working from home, some employees demonstrate increasing withdrawal from their actual work. In addition, some employers claimed that employees who work from home and are using smartphones often put least effort particularly in crafting job-related messages since it is easy to send. This scenario brings lack of nonverbal cues in communicating job-related messages.

Subsequently, while from home, some employees lose track of their tasks and responsibilities, particularly when a supervisor makes an autonomous decision. Autonomous decisions happen when a directive is carried out fully through email or text. Such directives make staff fail to foresee the brevity of the communication, which leads to confusion and missing important information for carrying out their tasks or, at times, feeling forgotten or left out.

With regard to cybersecurity, several employees are also exposed to threats while using technology from home, such as phishing during the pandemic lockdown. Generally, the issue on security while using technology from home is due to many factors. One of the key factors is that employees are unprepared and not fully trained to face the challenges since the lockdown happened all of a sudden. In addition, a lot of employees who are working from home end up leaving their computers on, which exposes it to enormous security risk. When young employees leave their computer on, this will invite their roommate to gain access to an unattended information.

Using multiple digital applications during work from home also made the employees feel exhausted. Since most of the meetings moved online during the pandemic lockdown, many employees suffered from Zoom fatigue, a phenomenon of emotional and physical drain caused by videoconferencing.

The challenges of using technology from home is also influenced by the readiness of employees to accept new applications, particularly applications that were drastically introduced during the pandemic lockdown. The complexity of the application makes the employees more stressful, which reduces their readiness behavior and motivation to learn.

Chapter 8

The Privileges of Working from Home during COVID-19 Pandemic Lockdown

Broadly, there are many privileges to working from home, although there is no doubt pertaining to the challenges in implementing the policy. Working from home indeed brings several privileges to both employers and employees. One of the profound reasons that explains the benefits of working from home to both employer and employee is job flexibility.

Viewing from employee perspective, job flexibility allows and gives them an opportunity to control both working hours and working time. Allowing them to control working hours and times has triggered several other subsequent opportunities. Firstly, it creates an environment in which employees can decide freely on their own working hours and time—of course, with the green light from the employers. Secondly, it gives job autonomy to employees on how to perform the job.

Explaining further on job autonomy, working from home allows employees to work during the most productive time, such as how they can decide when to start and when to finish their works. This will make it possible for them to establish a work rhythm that best suits their preferences, and furthermore, it reduces workplace distraction.

Having this privilege brings many psychological benefits to employees. Among the psychological benefits are employees feeling fulfilled, blessed, happy, and hassle-free with their choice. They are still earning money although they are staying at home. They do not have to worry about pressure from their colleagues, neither dress code nor decorum. There is also no need to wake up early or work late as long the tasks assigned to them are completed on time.

On the other hand, viewing from the employer perspective, job flexibility is on how an organization increases control through ongoing negotiation and engendering give-and-take approach while the employee is working from home. Practically, an organization may exercise some control at the initial stage of negotiation with employees but later reduce the grip once the specific form of flexibility has been agreed and signed on.

In a similar vein, by allowing employees to work from home, employers could also gain several other benefits, such as reduced real estate footprint, avoided unethical office politics among the employees, reduced employees' misconduct, minimized staff absenteeism, ability to hire the top talent without geographic limits, and finally, improved staff retentions.

The practice of working from home has obviously reduced real estate footprint. This scenario can be observed where the desk occupancy rate in the office has dropped to 50 percent. Unused office space means employers could save a lot of money on rental, maintenance, utilities, and other property-related expenses. By allowing employees to work from home, employers not only improve economic utilization of office space but also create agile workplace environment.

Since working from home constrained physical social interaction between the employees, it also could help to avoid unethical office politics, which is considered a harmful act to organizations. Unethical office practice manifests action by employees that are directed toward the goal of furthering their own self-interest without regard for the well-being of others or their organizations.

Among the behaviors spotted by the organization social scientists are employees' condemning and suppressing others, supervisors playing favorites, and coworkers sabotaging one another's work effort. In addition, it also includes employees having connection to top-management allies and playing powerful coalitions. All these unethical office politics behaviors, which harm the employers, have disappeared while employees are working from their home.

Similar to unethical office politics behavior, work from home also could bring several other advantages to employers;

for instance, employers could reduce employees' misconduct incidents, such as cheating, stealing, wrongdoing, and other different form of dishonesty. Some forms of dishonesty include taking office supplies without permission or using office telephone for personal business interests. While working from home, employees have no opportunity to get involved with this misconduct.

Reducing staff absenteeism is another advantage to employers while their employees are working from home. Leveraging technology allows employers to actively monitor attendance of employees who are working from home using artificial intelligence application, which is built in to employees' personal computers. This benefits many things such as tracking employee keystrokes, when they log in and log out, taking photographs with laptop camera to see if employees are present, and taking facial photographs to get a measure of how hard they are working based on facial expressions. To a certain extent, employers are reaching deep into employees' home to collect more data about their employees' attendance and other job-related activities.

Explaining further on benefit to employer, working-from-home policy enables employers to hire the top talent without geographic limits and save recruitment cost and cost per hire. In addition, working-from-home policy also allows employer to attract and retain the best talent from a large number of talent pool regardless of the locations.

Discussing further on the privilege of working from home to employee, several advantages have been discovered: better work-life balance, better work-family balance, reduced time of communication and commuting time, and save traveling expenses. Working from home also provides opportunity for employees to work even during sick leave, reduces work-to-home and home-to-work conflict, improves employees' performance productivity, helps environmental cleanliness, and reduces distance barrier.

Viewing particularly from the gender perspective, working from home brings more advantages to women employees compared to men employees. Apparently, working from home has been valued more by women than men since it helps women to take care of their household and children. In addition, it allows them to plan their work and plan their time. The motivation to work from home is also triggered by their long history doing both paid and unpaid labor from home.

With regard to work-life balance, since more employees are looking for a better work-life balance, the working-from-home policy during the COVID-19 pandemic lockdown has open a lot of benefits for them, in which they get a chance to remain in the workforce and continue to be employed by an established company yet also enjoy all the advantages of being at home. The employees seem to be attracted to employers who adopt the working-from-home policy and accept the fact that this is now becoming priority for employment. As such, the working-from-home policy has improved the employees' ability to manage work-life interplay.

In addition to work-life balance, the working-from-home policy has also improved work-family balance. Work-family balance allows employees not only to be with family members but also to create a family-friendly environment. The unique thing is that while they enjoy leisure time with family members, they are also earning at the same time. It was a choice they were proud of because they earned without compromising their family duties.

Working from home also acts as a strategy to allow employees to take care and nurture their dependents. For instance, employees who are involved in working from home spend their time with their children in the morning and have breakfast together, which would not be possible without working from home.

Since the cost of childcare is expensive, for some employees who have a large number of children, working from home is a great perk for them. This is proven based on the observations that study the synchronization between working from home and family perspective. Working from home also offers employees to take care of family members, such as parents and disabled family members. This opportunity is considered valuable sources of satisfaction for the employees.

In addition, working from home also reduces time for irrelevant communication and interaction, such as office gossiping and false assumptions, with colleague and coworkers.

This could offer extra time resources leading to higher productivity.

Highlighting mobility, working from home also has reduced commuting time for employees since they no longer need to travel to and from home. In addition, it also saves traveling expenses for employees.

In a similar vein, working from home offers employees to work in case of sickness. Being able to work from home in case of sickness can be considered as an alternative to workplace presenteeism, which is defined as "attending work while ill." Working from home makes it possible for those employees who wish to fulfill their work obligations under any circumstances with less stress. This opportunity could be considered as important resources, which increase employees' satisfaction.

Explaining further, working from home also has shown positive implication on employees' performance and productivity. This is due to the fact that employees who are working from home are at their creative best since they don't feel stress and, furthermore, don't worry about the morning traffic jam. Apparently, not all employees are at their creative best. While some are more productive at different times of the day, some are more productive on weekends. Working from home allows employees to contribute their works at the pace of their own creativity.

Chapter 9

Digital Technology as a Magic Bullet for Performing Work from Home during COVID-19 Pandemic Lockdown

The forceful nature of work from home has suddenly brought a number of disruptions on how the work is undertaken for a large number of employees and employers. The sudden work-from-home policy has pushed many employees and employers to leverage digital technologies as a solution to perform their tasks, duties, and responsibilities. Strengthening further, digital technology has been fully empowered and shifted to a high-speed gear with the objective to accomplish the working-from-home policy. Surprisingly, digital technologies have made the employees functioning well at home although they are away from the confine of normal workplaces or work hours.

Although using technology is not a new phenomenon at workplaces, the forceful and drastic nature of work from home during the COVID-19 pandemic lockdown has warned the employees that they have no option but rather to cope with its application. Contrarily, employees who are slow to integrate digital technology into their daily routine working from home were forced to adapt more rapidly. Work from home therefore encourages digital surge in every employee's career life. Borrowing a behavioral economist's quotation, *"Work from home gave all things digital."*

It is the expectation of employers, therefore, that employees capture the quick task-focused benefits of functions developed in digital technologies. There are many functions of digital technology that could help employees to perform their work efficiently from home. For instance, digital technologies provide more independence for employees to work from home. The interesting part is that this new form of independence offers employees the ability of working from home at any time.

In addition, no distance is needed to be bridged anymore to exchange information. Seemingly, digital technology allows employees to perform beyond physical formal office space, offers more choices, and boosts motivation and interest while working from home.

Broadly, digital technologies consist a group of powerful, accessible, and potentially game-changing applications—for instance, social mobile, cloud, analytics, Internet of Things, cognitive computing, and biometrics. Extending further, it is also known as digital connectivity via email, instant messaging services, Zoom, Skype, Google Meet, WeChat, webinar, smart HR technology, artificial intelligence technology, robotics, and digital marketing, which is enabled through tablets, smartphones, wearables, and others. Devices such as these have become an inherent part of working from home at all hours. The advantage is that employees who are working from home could engage not only with their own works but also with their work-related colleagues.

While working from home, employees have used digital technologies for multiple purposes, ranging from consultation to collaboration, transaction, and adoption of automation. Strengthening further, working from home encourages employees to use digital technology as a solution provider in many areas of their tasks. Among the tasks are to provide multiple solutions in health services, human resources activities, conducting meetings, conferences, projects monitoring, customer services, education, and training.

With regard to health solution, digital technology has been used amazingly by a large number of health workers, which we never ever imagined before. Working-from-home policy has shifted the health care system to become increasingly virtual through telehealth, telemedicine, artificial intelligence, and internet of other things. Explaining telehealth, it encourages, for instance, registered dietitian nutritionists to deliver nutrition care to their patients without seeing them physically. On the other hand, telemedicine digital technology encourages health care workers to convert their outpatients to virtual modalities either by telephone or video while working from home. Surprisingly, using a tablet, patients who are admitted are able to interact with health workers from their homes.

The most profound health solution, however, provided by digital technology to health workers while working from home is artificial intelligence. Artificial intelligence has been used to track the movement of the COVID-19 virus to conduct online doctor-to-patient consultation, to deliver medical supplies, and to recognize faces that are not wearing masks.

With regard to tracking, hospital personnel are able to locate the COVID-19 virus at real time even without going to the field. For instance, artificial intelligence technology is able to predict where the virus might appear next and to detect whether people had the virus based on visual sign of COVID-19 on a lung CT scan. Strengthening further, artificial intelligence technology is also able to monitor real-time changes in body temperature through the use of wearable sensors and to provide an open-source data platform to track the spread of the disease.

In addition, artificial intelligence technology is also being used to conduct online doctor-to-patient consultation to support the emergency cases. The interesting part is that the artificial technology is able to classify the medical image of the patient, which prompted health care workers to manage patient diseases just by doing it from home.

Explaining further on the role of artificial intelligence, it is also used to deliver medical supplies by drone to recognize faces that don't wear mask in public and to disinfect patient rooms while the hospital personnel is working from home. It is also able to detect fake news about the disease by applying machine-learning techniques for mining social media information and tracking down words that are sensational and alarming to government authority.

Using other digital technology, such as Internet of Things devices, health personnel can monitor patient progress using smartphone from home—for instance, early detection of functional vision impairment for diabetic patients. Amazingly, all these tasks could be perform from home without attending in hospital premises.

Similar to provide health solution, work from home also encourages employees to use digital technologies to provide human resource solution. Among the digital technologies used include artificial intelligence, videoconferencing, gig economy, and smart human resource technologies. The great advancement is that artificial intelligence is used to manage not only employees' attendance but also to track their performance while they are working from home. Elaborating further on employees' attendance, artificial intelligence technology—through keystroke, which is built in to employees' laptop—allows employer to actively monitor employees' punch in and punch out.

The keystroke also allows employers to track employees' performance when they log in and log out, taking photographs with the laptop camera to see if employees are doing their work at the workstation, and taking facial photographs to get a measure of how hard they are working based on facial expressions. Amazingly, to a certain extent, employers are reaching deep into employees' home to collect more data about their employees' attendance and performance.

Other digital technology that is used to provide human resource solution while employees are working from home is video conferencing. Through the application of video conferencing, employees can be monitored on the job constantly. Video conferencing makes it easier for bosses and managers to call and locate subordinates at any time knowing that they can be reached at all time. In addition, using gig economy allows HR managers to hire workers on ad hoc, short-contract, and informal basis while the former's working from home.

Subsequently, smart technology is also being used to provide human resource solution while employees are working from home. Smart human resource management technologies are defined as the digital revolution in task activities that are executed in a manner that depends somewhat on cloud computing, big data, and automation.

Leveraging smart human resource management technologies allows employees not only to perform and complete digital tasks independently but also, interestingly, it allows them to engage digitally with their immediate superiors, subordinates, and coworkers from home. Elaborating further on digital engagement, it allow employees to give directive to subordinate and similarly received command from their superiors using social media.

Work from home also encourages employees to use digital technology, such as Zoom application to run the meeting and conferencing activities. Apparently, employees who are working from home have turned their spotlight on Zoom application to run video meeting and conferencing like never before. Using Zoom applications from home, the conduct of the meeting has been digitized using SMART Boards instead of whiteboards.

Zoom Cloud Meetings also enable employees to exchange information and do presentation, calculation, and simulation. In addition, Zoom cloud meetings make possible to arrange meeting between people not colocated and transmit information between people over time. Different meetings can be conducted between different home and time—for instance, same time and different home, different time and different home. As a result, there is no hassle to conduct meeting while employees are working from home.

Highlighting managing project, work from home encourages employees to use WeChat accounts without going to the field site. Quoting employees' experience using WeChat accounts, millions of employees manage to transfer work files, track project progress, and manage leave request, which suggests they are always on engagement with their work colleagues although they are working from home. WeChat digital technology has empowered employees to perform their works even if they are physically distanced from one another and from the office.

Highlighting entrepreneurial field, work from home encourages business operators to use e-good technology to provide solution to customer services. Using e-good has resulted in more fluid entrepreneurial works from home. As such, the transformational effect of e-good technology has boosted further the motivations and interests of entrepreneurs to work from home. Amazingly, the application of e-good as an enabler while working from home has improved entrepreneurial activities.

Among the e-goods are online storefronts such as Magento and Shopify and online marketplaces such as Amazon Marketplace, eBay, Etsy, and Alibaba. In addition, it includes advancement of trading opportunities by social media such as Facebook, online payment such as PayPal and Square, and drop shipping, which avoids the need for inventory while working from home.

Similarly, work from home encourages teachers, lecturers, professors, professional trainers, and toastmasters to deliver their teachings, lectures, seminars, conferences, research findings, trainings, and workshops to their students, participants, and trainees. Surprisingly, they used multiple digital applications to realize the learning outcomes.

Although there are many digital technologies to facilitate the learning outcomes, the most prominent applications are Zoom, webinar, and Google Meet. In addition, it includes instant messaging applications, such as WhatsApp, Twitter, and Telegram. All these applications provide solutions to education and training although facilitators are doing their work from home.

Highlighting education broadly, it has experimented a dramatic shift to the online mode of transacting, where all the academic staff control the learning process from their homes. Since the beginning of working from home, schools, colleges, and university teachers and academic staff have shifted their classes to video conferencing platforms like Zoom, webinar, Google Meet, and instant messaging.

Highlighting Zoom specifically, it is the most contemporary digital technology applied by academicians. The application of Zoom experienced a surge, and according to Zoom Blog (2020), its user base jumps over three hundred million daily. Zoom bombing attracted a large number of academicians from a large number of universities.

Undergraduate and postgraduate university students heavily use the Zoom application to deliver their academic assignment, proposal defense, candidature defense, and even PhD viva, while all the lecturers, professors, and scholars monitor it from their homes.

Similarly, webinar is another digital tool that is applied in higher education. Webinars are defined as web-based seminars in which students and lecturers communicate live over the internet synchronously in real time using web camera and voice over IP. Generally, it offers screen sharing, videos, slides, chats, questions and answers, polls, virtual room for group work, and real-time feedback among students and lecturers. At the end of webinar events, lecturers can perform follow-up analysis and evaluation of webinar classes.

In addition to higher learning education, work from home also has forced school teachers to teach young generation using the Google Meet application. The school days consist two to four live sessions a day via Google Meet. After an approximately twenty-minute live session, students have forty to fifty minutes for individual work. The class will gather again for a live session using Google Meet after students complete their works. At the end of the school day, the teachers check children's daily tasks in, for example, Google Classroom and start to plan together the lessons of the next days. Apparently, all these tasks have been done from home without need for the teachers to attend the physical classroom.

Similar to school teachers, work from home also has forced professional medical trainers to conduct online education that does not require them to attend training rooms in the hospitals. Among the digital technologies applied to realize the learning program is Zoom and webinar applications. Webinars allow trainee doctors to present seminars and participate using their own computer or mobile device. Multiple fields of medical disciplines have been delivered from home, such as surgical training, neurosurgery, postgraduate medical education, dermatology, and plastic and reconstructive surgery.

Chapter 10

Work-from-Home Policy and Employees' Job Manual—a Practical Guideline for Human Resource Managers and Employees

Since working from home was mandated for both employers and employees during the COVID-19 pandemic lockdown, there was no crystal clear human resource policy that specifically explained this working condition. Although some companies have been practicing working from home long ago, the policy is still vague and needs modification with the current pandemic situation to ensure job preservation.

Similarly, from the employee perspective, there is no practical job manual written so far to guide employees on work from home. Practically, employees are still stressed and confused with the dramatic and sudden change of workplace.

Both working-from-home written policy for human resource managers and employees' job manual will guide them in implementing working from home.

In a normal practice before the pandemic, the work-from-home policy was implemented voluntarily between employers and employees, which required both parties to sign the agreement. However, the current work-from-home policy is forceful and unique, which is designed as a temporary measure. The sole objective of the current work-from-home policy is to minimize the spread of COVID-19; therefore, employers and employees must fully comply with all the health requirements. There are many companies who practice the work-from-home policy for the first time, and the challenge is they need to quickly and urgently adopt the work arrangement.

While there is no one-size-fits-all working-from-home policy, a general guideline that explains the modus operandi must be issued by the human resource department. The working-from-home policy should cover the main components of the policy and other additional elements for consideration to face the different needs of the company.

When preparing the work-from-home policy, human resource managers should take into consideration several important procedures that should be included in the policy. Broadly, it should include the *objective*, definition, entitlement, effective date, existing employment condition, and employees' and employers' responsibilities.

With regard to *objective*, human resource managers should explain that working from home is not a formal entitlement or special perk but rather a temporary measure to face the emergency situation of the COVID-19 pandemic lockdown enforced by the government. They should also emphasize that the working-from-home policy is subject to change as the situation develops in the future. By explaining the *objective*, it will reduce the tension, confusion, or hiccup among the employees.

In interpreting the work-from-home policy, it is the responsibility of human resource managers to make a special reference on the legal aspect since different countries have different legal implications. However, the general definition should explain that work from home is a working arrangement in which employees use digital technology yet perform major tasks and fulfill essential work responsibilities.

Highlighting effectiveness of the working-from-home policy, it is important to brief its effective date as suggested by the authority. In addition, it should also explain who is entitled and who is not entitled. The reason is because there are some works that must be done from office premise, particularly work that involves security. In many cases, security and safety personnel are not entitled since they are the frontliners in the organization. However, at the end of the day, it is the discretion of human resource managers to decide who is entitled and who is not entitled to work from home.

In addition, it is also important to take note that while preparing the work-from-home policy, human resource managers should highlight that the policy does not change or replace the employment terms and conditions of the employees and make sure the employees fully understand all the procedural matters pertaining to the policy. Subsequently, the work-from-home policy also should strengthen that there is no changes in the employees' compensation.

Explaining further about the employment condition of the policy, human resource managers should add a special clause that the company has the right to change, modify, and discontinue the arrangement for any workers at any time as it deems fit. This is to secure the company from any misuse of the working-from-home policy by some irresponsible employees.

With regard to employees' responsibilities, human resource managers should also highlight in the work-from-home policy that although the employees are working from home, their compliance with work while they are performing from home is similar with their compliance while they are working from office. This includes compliance on working hours, responsibilities, occupational safety and health, use of ICT, data protection, confidentiality, intellectual property, and company code of conduct. Other things that they should comply with are the usage of company laptop, software, tools, equipment, social media, antidiscrimination, anti-harassment, and equal opportunity.

The employee is also responsible for following the instruction given by the company on establishing and maintaining designated workplace in a healthy, safe, professional, and secure manner. The work-from-home policy also must state that in case of any remodeling, electrical modification, and office improvement needs by the employee, they must obtain prior approval from the company.

In addition, the policy also should state the use of equipment, software, data supplies, and furniture provided by the company is for use by the employees and relating to company business only. Furthermore, the policy also should mention that it is the responsibility of employees to take a good care of all the tools provided by the company and contact their managers if there is an issue with regard to equipment, software, or connectivity.

Elaborating on communication, the work-from-home policy should state that it is the responsibility of employees to make themselves accessible to their managers and coworkers during the agreed working hours and how they could be contacted using ICT. In any case of illness, injury, accident, or lockdown, employees must notify the immediate supervisors.

Similarly, the policy also should state the responsibility of employees to maintain a performance standard that is expected to be similar by the employer while the former are working from office. In addition, the employees are expected to maintain professionalism while working from home.

Viewing from employer perspective, working from home requires full support from the companies. For instance, employers should not change the employment conditions of the employees, particularly on compensation, perks, salaries, bonus, leave entitlement, and any other benefits that employees deserve.

The work-from-home policy also should highlight that all equipment and tools employees need to carry out their work from home should be provided by the company. This includes mobile phone, hardware, software, access to internet, access to host application, and internet cost.

When designing the work-from-home policy, human resource managers should elaborate that the company is responsible concerning the cost associated with home office setup, equipment installation, and safety at employees' home. However, the layout of the home office should be provided by the employees based on procedures stated by the company. The work-from-home policy also must state that any remodeling, electrical modification, and office improvement must obtain prior approval from the company.

Since employees' home workspace is considered an extension of employers' work-from-home arrangement, the policy should highlight that any injury or accident that'll occur to employees arising from the employment during the working hours is the responsibility of the employers. Therefore, the work-from-home policy should highlight in detail the responsibility of the employers with regard to the injury that'll occur to employees.

The work-from-home policy should also elaborate how the employees' performance appraisal is measured to give fair judgment to the employees. Thus, the work-from-home policy should highlight similar indicators used by employers while managing them physically. This is to avoid discrepancy pertaining to the result of the employees. Employers' responsibilities—such as communicating clear goals and tracking employees' progress and mobility—should be taken into consideration while preparing the working-from-home policy.

The work-from-home policy should consider cybersecurity and privacy issues, particularly on the responsibilities of employers to take care of data security and to provide robust information technology system in place, safe transmission of data outside of workplace, installation of proper software, antivirus protection, and secured virtual private network. The reason is because during the pandemic lockdown, millions of data and files are being transferred.

Explaining further on the content of the working-from-home policy, it should also take note of the employers' responsibility to provide official working hours to control the availability of the employees at their workstation from home. However, it should be based on national legislation, collective agreement, and company rules.

In addition to comprehensive work-from-home policy for human resource managers, an employees' job manual that guides employees to work from home will clear the hiccup and confusion. The employees' job manual that outlines how they are going to face work from home can be divided into two broad areas. It includes ability to draw a clear line between domain of work and home and usage of available technological tools.

Explaining further on the ability to draw a clear line between domain of work and home, it will help the employees to set a boundary to avoid interrole conflict. For instance, role of work will not penetrate into role of home and vice versa. In addition, it will reduce employees' burnout, tension, and stress, which leads to high productivity and job performance. To achieve this, employees—with the help of human resource personnel—should strategize three initiatives. It includes how to create a space just for work, keep a schedule, and avoid mixing work and housework.

Creating a space just for work needs comfortable chairs and tables. Having an office with a door that closes makes a huge difference. A proper work schedule that is provided by the human resource department to all employees will be helpful. Full utilization of working schedule through digital technologies provided by companies will help employees to avoid mixing up work and housework.

The employees' job manual should list all the digital technologies available for employees. The job manual should also list IT personnel names and contact numbers to avoid connectivity problem that may occur while the employees are working from home. Meeting is one of the essential job activities that regularly occur between employees and their managers. This requires very powerful tools such as Zoom, webinar, and Skype, which is provided by the employer together with password.

Similarly, other useful digital tools that are required by employees while working from home, include such as artificial intelligence. Artificial intelligence will motivate employees to work from home since it has a very powerful ability in monitoring employees' attitudes, performance, and attendance. On the other hand, instant messaging—such as Facebook, WhatsApp, and Telegram—is useful tool for interstaff communication. All in all, listing all these applications in the employees' job manual will somehow motivate the employees to work from home.

www.ingramcontent.com/pod-product-compliance
Lightning Source LLC
Chambersburg PA
CBHW030847180526
45163CB00004B/1482